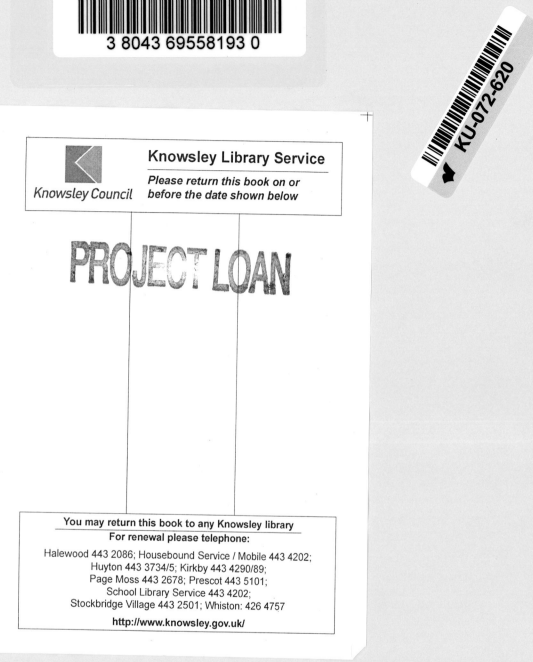

Knowsley Library Service

Please return this book on or before the date shown below

Knowsley Council

PROJECT LOAN

Discover and Share

Pets

Angela Royston

FRANKLIN WATTS
LONDON • SYDNEY

About this book

The **Discover and Share** series enables young readers to read about familiar topics independently. The books are designed to build on children's existing knowledge while providing new information and vocabulary. By sharing this book, either with an adult or another child, young children can learn how to access information, build word recognition skills and develop reading confidence in an enjoyable way.

Reading tips

 Begin by finding out what children already know about the topic. Encourage them to talk about it and take the opportunity to introduce vocabulary specific to the topic.

Each image is explained through two levels of text. Confident readers will be able to read the higher level text independently, while emerging readers can try reading the simpler sentences.

Check for understanding of any unfamiliar words and concepts. Inexperienced readers might need you to read some or all of the text to them. Encourage children to retell the information in their own words.

 After you have explored the book together, try the quiz on page 22 to see what children can remember and to encourage further discussion.

Contents

Words in **bold** are in the glossary on page 23.

What is a pet?

A pet is a tame animal that usually lives in your home. Tame animals are not afraid of people.

There are lots of different kinds of pet. Hamsters are small. This dog is a Great Dane. It is very big!

Pets live with us. Some pets are small, but some are big.

Looking after a pet

Wild animals look after themselves, but pets need people to look after them.

Pets need clean water to drink and food to eat. They need space to exercise and clean **bedding** to sleep in.

You need to take care of a pet. Pets need clean water to drink.

Friendly dogs

Dogs like to go for walks.
They wag their tail when
they are happy.

Dogs like to go for a long walk every day. If you throw a ball, the dog will run after it.

You can tell how a dog feels. When it is happy it holds its tail up high and wags it from side to side.

9

Cool cats

Cats like to spend time on their own, but they also like to be stroked. They may **purr** when they are stroked.

Cats chase anything that moves quickly, such as a toy mouse or a ball.

Some cats
purr when
they are
stroked.

Rabbits in the garden

This rabbit lives in the garden. It likes to eat the grass.

Many pet rabbits live outside in the garden.
They have a special **hutch** to shelter in.

Rabbits nibble the grass and keep it short.   13

Hamster home

A hamster likes a cage
with lots of space
to play.
The cage
keeps the
hamster safe.

The hamster has everything
it needs in the cage. It sucks
water from a special water bottle.

A hamster is safe in its cage.
It has all the things
it needs here.

Hungry lizards

Some people keep lizards as pets.
A lizard is a type of **reptile**.
A reptile's skin is covered with
hard **scales**.

A lizard eats insects, such as **crickets**.
It also likes pieces of vegetable and fruit.

**A lizard has
scaly skin.
It eats insects
and fruit.**

17

Fish tank

Lots of different pet fish live together in a tank.

Fish eat special fish **pellets.** When pellets are dropped into the water, the fish come to the surface to eat them.

Lots of fish live in this tank.
The fish swim up to get the food.

Visiting the vet

Sometimes a pet becomes ill. Then you have to put your pet in a special **carrier** and take it to a vet.

The vet may give your pet medicine to make it better.

Pets sometimes get ill. You should take them to a vet.

Quiz

1. What is this cat doing?

2. How does a dog show it is happy?

3. What does this rabbit like to eat?

4. How many fish can you see in this picture?

Glossary

bedding dried grass or other material which animals sleep on

carrier a cage or basket for carrying something

cricket a jumping insect

hutch a cage designed for rabbits

pellets small pieces of a mixture of many types of food

purr gentle growling sound made by a cat

reptile a large group of animals which have a dry, scaly skin. Snakes and lizards are reptiles.

scales small pieces of hard skin

wild not owned or looked after by people

Answers to quiz:
1. It is drinking water.
2. It wags its tail.
3. Grass.
4. Three.

23

Index

First published in 2013 by
Franklin Watts
338 Euston Road
London
NW1 3BH

Franklin Watts Australia
Level 17/207 Kent Street
Sydney
NSW 2000

Copyright © Franklin Watts 2013

HB ISBN 978 1 4451 1731 7
Library ebook ISBN 978 1 4451 2499 5

Dewey number: 636'.0887

A CIP catalogue record for this book is
available from the British Library.

Series Editor: Julia Bird
Series Advisor: Karina Law
Series Design: Basement68

Picture credits: Ermolaev Alexander /Shutterstock: 11. Arco/Nature PL: 13.
Yuri Arcurs/Dreamstime: 4, 17, 23. Art Directors and Trip/Alamy: 15. Breti
Critchley/Dreamstime: 18. Eldacarin/Dreamstime: 3b, 9. Imageman/
Shutterstock: 12, 22bl. Tatiana Katsai/Shutterstock: front cover.
Lusoimages/Shutterstock: 20. Julia Mashkova/istockphoto: 7, 22tl.
Mkoudis/Dreamstime: 2, 6. Guy Moberly/Alamy: 8, 22tr.
Papilio/Alamy: 3c, 14. Artem and Olga Sapegin/Shutterstock: 5.
Benjamin Simeneta/Dreamstime: 1, 10. Brocke Whatnall/Shutterstock:
3t, 16. Glenn Young/Shutterstock: 19, 22br.

Printed in China

Franklin Watts is a division of
Hachette Children's Books,
an Hachette UK company.
www.hachette.co.uk